Gianna Mago is extremely passionate about sports, especially football. Her skills on the field have won her many awards. She also has a knack for writing captivating stories.

Besides football, Gianna loves the outdoors and is immensely fond of dogs. Gianna has set her sights on a unique and an exciting career path—film direction, which helps her to express her creativity through a different medium. With passion, dedication, determination and a string of achievements under her belt, Gianna is poised to make a mark in the world.

Gianna is currently studying Film Studies in New York.

YOU GOT THIS!

The Art of Loving Yourself

Gianna Mago

Om Books International

Reprinted in 2025

Om Books International

Corporate & Editorial Office
A-12, Sector 64, Noida 201 301
Uttar Pradesh, India
Phone: +91 120 477 4100
Email: editorial@ombooks.com
Website: www.ombooksinternational.com

Sales Office
107, Ansari Road, Darya Ganj,
New Delhi 110 002, India
Phone: +91 11 4000 9000
Email: sales@ombooks.com
Website: www.ombooks.com

ISBN: 978-81-19750-16-0

Printed in India

10 9 8 7 6 5

To
Mom and Dad

Thank you for being my pillars of strength. In every stage of my journey, you two have always stood by me with immeasurable love, patience, guidance and the encouraging words, "You got this!" Your unstinted support has helped me be the courageous, caring and compassionate person I am today.

Thanks, Mom for teaching me with your nurturing spirit and wisdom the art of loving myself. If not for your gentle reminders that I should make time for myself, breathe and recharge in times of turmoil, I would have crumbled altogether. You have never stopped believing in me and gently steered me towards self-discovery and personal growth.

DAD, YOU ROCK! Your life is an example that courageous engagement with the world is an endeavour worthy of pursuit. Your sagacity shines through in this book.

My life is not an isolated case; it is just one of the many cases, and I want my experiences to guide and support other people out there who are suffering in the same way.

I write this book with a heart overflowing with love.

Contents

Introduction

Mental well-being is a prerequisite for overall well-being. It is not a luxury; in fact, it is a necessity. When you feel good in your mind, it positively affects your body as well. However, Indian society is still lagging behind when it comes to mental health awareness and acceptance of people dealing with such issues. People are hesitant to talk about their struggles with mental health with their close ones as it still considered a taboo by many. However, the brain is a part of the human body and can at times fall sick. This is when treatment is required so that one can recover from it.

It needs to be understood that suffering from a mental health issue is not a sign of weakness. In fact, the people who are struggling with it but still show up day in and day out and complete their tasks to the best of their abilities are truly brave souls who deserve to be appreciated. It requires unbelievable levels of strength, fortitude and courage to get out of bed when you are grappling with an issue that can be debilitating at times.

However, with the Covid-19 pandemic, mental health has started to get more media attention. Many celebrities and social media influencers seem to "cash in" on what they consider to be the latest "trend". But this is of little consequence to the masses who continue to suffer in silence and ignominy.

It needs to be understood that there is no shame in asking for help when you are suffering from a mental health problem. However, when doing so, do ensure that you are taking help from a qualified professional. Also, while undergoing any form of therapy, be completely open about the issues you are facing, so that the practitioner is fully aware of the extent of the problem and can share the necessary steps and treatment to ensure complete recovery.

Just like crops require suitable conditions to grow, similarly people also need to be in the right frame of mind to be able to achieve personal growth. Working on oneself requires consistent and regular effort. It is anything but a one-time investment. It cannot be predicted when the result of such efforts will be seen, hence it is important to stay on the path one has set for oneself.

When embarking on the journey of self-discovery and self-improvement, you need to realise that your uniqueness should be cherished and maintained. You should never aspire to copy someone else because by doing so you can potentially lose track of your own individual qualities and quirks which make you distinctive and special. Similarly, as you progress towards your goal, you must avoid comparisons with others and instead remember how you were in the past and appreciate how far you have come.

Nobody is perfect. As human beings, we are all fallible. This is something that you need to acknowledge. Hence, instead of pulling yourself down, you should analyse where you went wrong and how you can avoid repeating the mistake. This requires having a calm and analytical mind, which can be acquired with regular practice of techniques such as mindfulness and meditation.

Your level of physical fitness also has a bearing on your mental capabilities. Various studies have shown that exercising regularly has positive effects on the brain. It is said that doing regular workouts increases blood flow to the brain, improving concentration and productivity. In the long term, exercise has also been said to act like a natural anti-depressant. That being said, if someone is currently suffering from an illness like depression which requires them to take regular medication, it should be taken as per the instructions of the mental health professional. If at all the dosage has to be reduced, it must be done under the supervision and guidance of a psychiatrist because stopping such medication abruptly can be detrimental.

Finally, remember that self-love is an art that you must practise every day. There will be times that you may question yourself and the direction in which you are headed. In these moments, do not worry or panic. It is absolutely normal to have self-doubts. Instead, remember your past victories where you overcame odds which at the time seemed insurmountable. Remembering the times when you succeeded will act as a much-needed boost. You can also maintain a diary wherein you can list all of your accomplishments so far. It does not matter if it is big or small, each win counts. So, in those moments when you have failed or fallen short, remember that you are human. We fall down, get back up and live to fight another day. This is life. It is a never-ending cycle of learning and growing. It is said that a journey of a thousand miles starts with a single step. And you, my friend, have taken a step in the right direction by reading this book.

1
What Makes You *You*?

The journey of self-discovery is a long and an arduous one. Hence, very few people embark on this expedition and even fewer actually find the answer they set out in search of. This journey requires incredible levels of focus, decisive action and above all, dedication and commitment. It must be kept in mind that you cannot make a change without putting in the work.

Path to self-discovery

Self-discovery is the process of understanding your true self, your values, your needs and wants. We have naturally discovered and learnt various qualities about ourselves over time. However, a significant number of people lose touch of their values and preferences once they realize that life involves endless work, errands to run and commitments to uphold. Our busy routines filled with hustle and bustle rarely give us the time to sit and contemplate on the life we actually want to live. Along the way, the need for self-discovery gets pushed into the background and is slowly forgotten.

Introspect

The first step to finding out who you are is to introspect. Unless you do not explore who you are, you will not know anything about yourself. You need to find things that make you happy, for instance, going out for a walk with your dog or watching the sunrise with someone you love. Unless you step out of your comfort zone, step out into the world and face challenges, you will never know who you are. Remember, the only thing constant in your life is change. Over time, many things like your behaviour, your friends will change, but one thing that never really changes is your nature. *Our true, intrinsic nature is something that remains constant.*

As you go along this path, you will learn new things about yourself, some of which would be exciting and fascinating while others may be disappointing and gut-wrenching. In such times, you will need courage and resilience to stick with the process despite the frustration and despair. To find what truly makes you *you*, requires you to dig deep and have a serious look inwards. It means finding out who you are as a person and a human being. Your love for dogs, sports or cooking does not define you. Your thoughts, values and principles are some things you will realise over the course of this journey, which is a continuous process. Who you are is also not constant and is subject to change depending on the people surrounding you, the circumstances and also the state of mind you are in while going through the situations.

Take out time every day to contemplate on what you have done that day. More importantly, try to analyse what you felt and thought as you did what you did. This will help you analyse your thought process, an integral ingredient in getting to know yourself. For best results, this process of deep contemplation and looking inwards should be done regularly. While you may be tempted to give it a miss because of your busy schedule, try to remember why you got started on this journey in the first place. Remind yourself how you felt at that time when you realised you needed answers without which you felt a panging you simply could not describe.

As you slowly start peeling through the layers, you will begin to find out about your true self. Do not rush through the process. Everyone takes their own time—some take days, others weeks while there may be those who may take months on end till they reach a conclusion. This requires an immense amount of dedication and self-discipline. There will be days when you will not find any answer and also times when answers will come to you easily. That is part and parcel of the process and should be embraced whole-heartedly. But remember that no matter how long and arduous the journey, it can be completed by only one way—*by taking one small step at a time*. So, stick to it and remember how far you have come and keep yourself motivated.

Keep a journal

If you are one of those who is struggling to find ways to discover who you truly are, a routine should be followed. Following a routine has immensely helped me when I was struggling.

Get a journal or download a voice recording app on your smartphone. Journaling has massive benefits. Many successful people like Albert Einstein were known to keep a journal to record their experiences, thoughts or feelings. Once you have written down your goals, you can keep track of your growth and progress and get to know how far you have come along. However, do make it a point to make your goals specific, realistic and time bound. Your goals should motivate you to act. They should not be so easy that they do not require any effort to achieve, nor should they be so challenging that you feel clueless and wonder where to begin in the first place. As you continue journaling on a consistent and regular basis, you will start seeing improvements in your thoughts and mindset and that will give you a much-needed boost of confidence which will reinvigorate you and inculcate a habit of consistency. Before you realise it, your writing and communication skills will see a significant improvement. The more you write and journal, your ability to express yourself will improve and this in turn will help during your social interactions as well.

Journaling is a great way to vent your anger, frustration and disappointments. You will notice that the negative thoughts which earlier would go on uncontrolled in your brain and at times were debilitating and demotivating, will now be easier to deal with. This will be especially helpful in stressful and challenging situations, which can be exhausting. But when you start penning down your thoughts and emotions on paper, you will realise that negative thoughts in your mind will be easier to manage and within some time will not be a hindrance to you. Such thoughts which were a cause of stress and worry for you, will cease to be so. As you mature, you will realise that as you write, you will find solutions by yourself without any help from anyone else. Also, as you journal over many months and years, you will have a treasury of information on how you dealt with the various issues which came your way. This will show you that majority of the problems have a workable solution. Glancing through these solutions in times of distress will give you tips on how to deal with your current predicament.

Prepare a to-do list

Take out time daily to plan what you are going to do the following day. This helps to give a structure to your day and brings a sense of comfort as you know what to expect and how to tackle the items on your to-do list. Preparing a to-do list helps to increase your productivity and motivation, reduces mental stress and anxiety and, most importantly, provides a sense of accomplishment when each task is completed successfully.

However, the list of items should not be too long or short and neither should they be too difficult or easy to accomplish. Ensure that there is a healthy mix of easy and difficult tasks so that you can keep yourself fresh and active throughout the day. The to-do list should not be daunting and should not induce a sense of stress or fear in you. Divide the big tasks into smaller ones. Also, divide the tasks in the following way—*important but not urgent; important and urgent; critical.*

This methodology helps you know which task you should tackle first.

The tasks that are critical, important and time-bound need to be dealt with first because it involves a timeline beyond which working on the task may not be possible, for example, if you have to visit the bank for something you have to do so during the banking hours. So, after these time-bound tasks are completed, it will free up your day to complete the rest of the tasks. While doing these tasks, you will be able to take your time without rushing yourself. And finally, after all your tasks for the day are completed, create a fresh to-do list with the same focus.

When you accomplish everything that you set out to do, remember to treat yourself. It does not matter if your accomplishments are big or small. What matters is that you had the willpower and discipline to go through with each and every one of them. Hence, it is good to pat yourself on the back and enjoy the success. Never think that you do not deserve something just because what you have achieved may seem small because successful completion of multiple small tasks will one day manifest into a gigantic success.

Remember to be as honest to yourself as you can. While we all try to hide things even from ourselves, such acts later on lead to a feeling of guilt which is an emotion that is unproductive. Be open to yourself and accept your faults and mistakes. Take the time to work on them so that you can become a better person.

There will be times, situations and people who will drag you away from truly finding yourself. Learn to push such people away. There will always be some people who will be detrimental to your growth. It is important to identify such people and distance yourself from them. Distancing yourself from a person for your self-growth and development is not something you should be ashamed of. It takes a truly brave and self-aware person to know what works for them.

Also, learn to be honest to yourself about how you feel. Do not be afraid to admit to yourself if you are feeling tense, worried, weak or stressed out. We are humans and feeling such negative emotions is normal and not something to be ashamed of.

Finally, learn to listen to your instincts. If you are not okay with something, do not convince yourself otherwise. Not acknowledging my gut feeling was one of the biggest mistakes I made in my life. Our instincts are like our guardian angels, protecting us from danger. Hence, they never lie to us. So, learn to trust your gut feeling because it will never fail you.

As I said before the journey to self-discovery is long, but can be incredibly fulfilling and satisfying. I really hope that this helps you in finding your true self and leads you to being contented, happy and successful in life.

2
How To Manage Overthinking

While overthinking, the mind goes through various scenarios, both actual and imaginary, over long periods of time. Your focus and concentration go for a toss and you find yourself losing track of time once you get caught in this vicious cycle. Overthinking does not lead to a solution of any kind. If uncontrolled, it can sap your mental and physical energy whereby you find it difficult to focus on anything of substance. As a result, your study, work and other daily activities can get hampered if this tendency is not managed properly. Research has shown that overthinking is associated with feelings of depression, anxiety and post-traumatic stress disorder (PTSD), issues which also need to be looked into and treated at the earliest to avoid complications in the future.

Signs of overthinking

Before we get into how to manage overthinking, let us look into the signs that you may be overthinking.

An inability to think about anything else

When you overthink, it occupies a major part of your mind space, making it extremely difficult to focus on anything else, as a result of which your daily tasks suffer.

Being unable to relax

The constant swirling of thoughts in your mind will mean that you are constantly feeling worried or anxious and will be unable to relax. Rest and recuperation are indispensable parts of life and ensure that you are fresh and alert to take on the next day. If your rest is inadequate over a long period of time, your productivity and focus will show a marked decline.

Feeling mentally exhausted

The uncontrolled stream of negative thoughts is debilitating and if unchecked can lead to mental fatigue, which in turn can result in burnout. Your thoughts have a manifestation on your physical well-being as well and such mental exhaustion can at times leave you feeling physically unwell.

Fixating on things outside of your control

There are some things that are out of your control such as what happened in the past and what will happen in the future. What is in your control is right now, the present. When overthinking takes over control, you will excessively fixate over anxieties of the past and worries about the future, which will lead to you being distracted in the present. This is not helpful as it leads to you becoming unproductive and also results in a decrease in quality and quantity of work output.

Having lots of negative thoughts

Most of the time, overthinking involves having an abundance of negative thoughts. Because of this, you keep on replaying negative situations or experiences in your mind, which can result in loss of confidence and self-esteem. In this negative state of mind, you constantly doubt yourself and second-guess your decisions. You may also lose hope and imagine and simulate all the worst-case scenarios in your mind.

Reasons behind overthinking

So why do we overthink? There are myriad of reasons behind this. Let us unpack a few of them:

Perfectionism

In an ideal world, we would all love to be perfect. But in reality, this is hardly the case. We all have our shortcomings and strengths. As you attempt to control every small detail and outcome of your life, you may get caught up in thinking about things that you cannot control and are outside your power. And this can snowball into an endless cycle of wasteful thoughts and energy. Once you break free from this vicious cycle, you will realise that perfectionism is actually unrealistic and impracticable.

Low self-esteem and negative thought patterns

If you have low self-esteem and diminished self-worth, you may be more prone to overthinking. Your habit of ruminating may get reinforced in case you have experienced some kind of trauma which has not been resolved, which can cause problems years after the initial traumatic event took place.

Excessive stress

Stress is an unpleasant emotion to experience. When you are experiencing it, your body gets tense and your mind goes on an overdrive. When you are under stress, your body and mind are under duress, which has a direct impact on your thoughts—both conscious and subconscious.

Uncertainty about the future

There may be times when your future may seem bleak or uncertain. Lack of clarity on the events of the coming days is also a cause of overthinking.

Lack of activity —an empty mind is the devil's workshop

This statement has remained relevant ever since humans came into existence. Our brain is like a muscle which should be exercised regularly to keep it fit, active and in good working condition. When you do not have anything constructive to do, it leads to your brain going into unproductive tangents which if unchecked can lead to overthinking. So, it is imperative that you keep yourself both mentally and physically active to keep your mind in control and keep overthinking at bay for as long as possible.

Procrastination

While the person indulging in procrastination may relax for some time, when the due date for completion of that activity comes close, they will experience an increase in stress and regret as to why they did not begin working on the task beforehand when they had sufficient time on their hands. Procrastination can adversely affect your output and productivity if it is not dealt with early on. Once procrastination becomes deeply ingrained in you, it is extremely difficult to hit the reset button and start afresh.

So, this brings us to the most important question of all: How to overcome overthinking?

How to manage overthinking

Let us discuss the ways to deal with overthinking.

Take a step back to observe your thoughts

Take stock of how you react to your thoughts. How do they affect you mentally, physically and emotionally? Do your thoughts make you feel irritated, weak or guilty? To do so requires having a good level of self-awareness. Thinking is not totally an unconscious act and it is something that we can control to a significant extent. You should be aware of your normal state of mind and how you think and react then. That should be the basis on which everything else should be compared. Make a note of how your body feels when you are in a good state of mind—usually your shoulders will be relaxed and your breath will be normal. Your heart beat will also be within normal parameters. You will feel a sense of calm and self-assurance and be confident that you will be able to handle most of the things that come your way with relative ease.

However, when you are in an agitated state of mind, your breath will be shallow and your body especially your shoulders will be tight and tense and you may experience dryness in your mouth and a sick feeling in the pit of your stomach, not to mention a quicker heartbeat. Once you notice that you are experiencing such symptoms, you should be able to take remedial actions to prevent serious health issues.

Do not take drastic and life-altering decisions

When we are in an agitated state of mind, we are not our normal self. Hence, our thought process will also be affected. So, in this disturbed state of mind, you should not take drastic life-altering decisions, which will affect your life and those around you in the long term. You must realise that while the moment may be debilitating, this stress shall pass.

Life is full of ups and downs. While it is easy to get swayed by the constant pendulum shift of our fortunes, you must realise that *this too shall pass—it is temporary*. While the bad times naturally will seem to be lasting longer than the good ones, it must be kept in mind that such favourable times will come back, sooner or later. During challenging times, try to persevere and remember the times in your life when you overcame problems and emerged successful. Such recalling of previous successes will reinvigorate you and boost your self-confidence, which will most definitely help you to face your present challenge with renewed enthusiasm, vigour and gusto.

Find a distraction

When you realise that you are overthinking, it is important that you break the vicious cycle of unproductive thoughts as soon as possible before it gets out of hand. To do so, involve yourself in some kind of activity such as:

Get into an exercise or workout routine

This diverts your attention from your thoughts towards the physical activity. Research has stated that taking part in regular physical activity increases blood flow to the brain which in turn improves mood regulation, concentration and productivity. In the long run, exercise can potentially act as a natural anti-depressant. After the workout, you will notice that you will feel better both in body and mind.

Learn a new skill or sharpen an existing skill

Learning a new skill such as cooking or painting will help you divert your mind when overthinking and will also be beneficial in the long term. Cooking is an important life skill and everyone irrespective of gender must ideally know their way around the kitchen to cook a decent meal for themselves when the need arises. If you already are someone who is a wizard in the kitchen, try to learn some new recipes to add to your repertoire which will help in impressing your family and friends.

Volunteer in a local organisation

Volunteering in a local organisation such as Rotaract Club will help you meet new people and gain a fresh perspective on life. Life can become boring and monotonous at home. Additionally, there is a greater chance of overthinking taking place if you are constantly within the four walls of your home. It is important to step out of the comfort zone of your home and into the world. Once you do that, your mind will get diverted and when you return home, you will feel reinvigorated.

Practise meditation and deep breathing

Meditation is a practice of focusing one's mind for a period of time, noticing but not engaging with thoughts. While doing such an activity, you will notice that loads of thoughts keep coming in your mind having the potential to distract you. It requires consistent practice to bring back your attention to a single thought by ignoring the ones that are trying to vie for your attention. While it may be frustrating initially, meditation and deep breathing are said to have incredible benefits for body, mind and soul in the long term.

Do something nice for someone

When you do something nice for someone it makes you feel at peace. You can help someone you know or take part in charitable activities to help the poor and needy. However, when doing so, ensure that you do adequate background research on the person/organisation needing the help and are convinced that the requirement is genuine and that your efforts or funds reach those in genuine need.

Ask for professional help

There is no shame in consulting a mental health professional as they are medically trained and know how to deal with various mental health issues and hence can give practical solutions, which untrained people may not be aware of. The brain at times may not be functioning to the best of its ability. In this scenario, a mental health professional will know exactly what needs to be done. However, when consulting such a professional, you need to ensure that they are genuine. Do the requisite background checks to satisfy yourself of their credentials. There are thousands of *mental health influencers* who post and comment about mental health. However, many of them do not have the professional degree or the training to treat mental health problems. So, keep this in mind before you select a mental health professional you would like to consult.

To conclude, you must keep in mind that as long as you are alive, you will have thoughts. It is impossible to stop them. However, you can decide which thoughts you want to give more attention to. Over time and with consistent and dedicated practice, you will pay attention to the thoughts that are truly important while ignoring the ones that you know are unproductive. The journey may be long and winding, but you will surely get there by taking one step at a time.

3
Understanding Happiness

The American Psychological Association (APA) defines happiness as "an emotion of joy, gladness, satisfaction and well-being". You will notice that when you experience these emotions, you do so for a few fleeting moments. So, in the moments when you do not feel even a single one of these emotions, are you an unhappy person? It is not so simple, right?

To expand, happiness can also be described as an emotional state characterised by feelings of joy, satisfaction, contentment and fulfilment. Irrespective of the various definitions, happiness usually involves experiencing and feeling positive emotions and life satisfaction. Because happiness is such a broad term, psychologists typically use the term *subjective well-being* when they talk about this emotional state.

What happiness is *not*

Before we delve into what happiness is, let us analyse what it is not:

Happiness is not feeling good all the time

Human beings experience a wide range of emotions. Our moods vary according to our circumstances, the time of the day, the kind of work or task we are engaged in and also the people accompanying us at the time. It is practically impossible to feel good all the time. Human nature is such that we experience mood swings rather regularly and as long as the fluctuations are not too serious or often it is completely normal to experience such ups and downs. According to researchers, having a calm state of mind and overall stable temperament is more beneficial to you than a mood in which you achieve great heights of happiness regularly.

Happiness is not the absence of problems

Life is challenging and at times it can overwhelm us. However, this does not mean that you cannot be happy. Problems are part and parcel of life and the best thing you can do is to accept them as smoothly as possible. With this attitude, the amount of discomfort you will feel when you experience problems will be reduced.

You may have often experienced that problems come up one after the other. If you are ready to accept and tackle them, the better it is for you. Happiness or more specifically, a general sense of contentment and satisfaction is something that can come despite problems. In fact, your sense of satisfaction will skyrocket when you will solve a problem or overcome an issue which you initially found to be daunting. Your self-confidence and self-worth will get a much-needed boost after you successfully overcome one challenge after another. So, you must learn how to co-exist with your problems and find a way to be contended despite their existence in your life.

Happiness is not being wealthy

Money is an important aspect of our lives and is vital for our existence in this world. While some may say that you must not find happiness in money, surviving without it is practically impossible in today's day and age. While not having money definitely makes life hard and being happy difficult, having money is not a sure-shot guarantee for happiness. You certainly will feel happy momentarily, but slowly and surely you will desire more money, more comforts that money can buy like cars, watches and new exciting destinations to travel, etc. This desire will keep increasing and frankly, there is no end to it. The more wealth you have, the more you will want and remain unsatisfied.

Happiness is not the "final destination"

I will be happy one day when I achieve or get ... This is based on the misconception that you will work towards becoming happy and one day will "arrive" there. Unless you are someone who is genetically predisposed to being happy, usually staying happy and maintaining a contented state of mind requires constant and consistent effort. So, while it may seem natural that you will be happy when you will pass an exam or get a job or promotion, this emotion is fleeting and will fade once you get used to them.

What is happiness?

So, *what is happiness*? The two key components of happiness or *subjective well-being* are:

The balance of emotions

Everyone experiences positive and negative emotions, feelings and moods. Happiness is generally linked to experiencing more positive feelings than negative ones.

Life satisfaction

This relates to your level of satisfaction with various aspects of your life like your work, relationships, achievements and other things you consider important.

One important thing to be noted is that *happiness is not a constant state of euphoria*. Instead, it is an overall sense of contentment whereby you experience more positive emotions than negative ones.

While perceptions of happiness may vary from one person to the next, there are some key signs that psychologists have identified while measuring and assessing happiness such as:

- Feeling like you are living the life you wanted.
- Going with the flow and a willingness to take life as it comes.
- Feeling that the conditions of your life are good.

- Enjoying positive, healthy relationships with other people.
- Feeling that you have accomplished (or will accomplish) what you want in life.
- Feeling satisfied with your life.
- Feeling more positive than negative.
- Being open to new ideas and experiences.
- Practising self-care and treating yourself with kindness and compassion.
- Experiencing gratitude.
- Feeling that you are living life with a sense of meaning and purpose.
- Wanting to share your happiness and joy with others.

This being said, people who are generally happy, still do face and experience negative emotions such as anger, sadness, despair, frustration, boredom and loneliness from time to time. But even when facing such uncomfortable emotions, there still is a deep sense of optimism and positivity which assures the person that things will get better and that they can adequately deal with what is happening to them and emerge stronger and happier.

Types of happiness

Diving deeper, let us explore the different types of happiness:

Joy

The feeling of joy is when you lose yourself in the present moment and appreciate what you have. It is a relatively accessible form of happiness as it can be found in many things if you have the right attitude, outlook and perspective. The easiest way to find joy is to engage in activities that you love.

Excitement

This emotion may be fleeting and can dissipate rather quickly. However, if harnessed effectively, it can be a motivating factor. For example, excitement of a new job or enrolling in a new course can motivate you to work harder than you otherwise would. The excitement can help you push through the difficulties that you may face in the initial days. It can also help you deal with nervousness that you may feel. Positive self-talk is extremely important and vital. If you tell yourself that you are excited instead of telling yourself that you are feeling nervous or worried, you can channel that uncomfortable energy into something positive and do some constructive activity.

Gratitude

Research has shown that those people who feel and experience gratitude on a regular basis tend to be happier and healthier than those less prone to these feelings. Luckily, the feeling of gratitude is rather simple and can be easily cultivated. The ways include using a gratitude journal, doing some kind of mindfulness meditation or even simply telling people in your life that you love and appreciate them. If you do this often, you will feel more grateful. Cultivating this feeling has been shown to ward off feelings of low self-worth and depression.

Optimism

Studies have shown that having an optimistic attitude is linked to greater success and positive outcomes in life. Optimists tend to focus on possibilities and have an attitude that includes both gratitude and pride. They are grateful for all of the possibilities life presents, proud of their abilities to harness these resources, and have a strong belief in themselves and their ability to achieve their goals. When faced with disappointment, optimists tend to minimise it and focus on how they can do better next time and find ways to mitigate factors that lead to negative outcomes. Optimists give themselves credit when they complete a job or task well and take it as a sign that better things are in store for them. Optimism being an attitude is more permanent and less fleeting than other forms of happiness.

Contentment

Contentment means being happy with what you have. While you may wish for more, the absence of those things does not decrease your sense of well-being and satisfaction. Those who are contented are less disappointed by life's drawbacks and feel grateful to have whatever they already have in their lives. This is something that many wise people strive towards. Enjoying your accomplishments to this point in your life can increase your sense of contentment.

So, when did you feel the happiest? This is different for each and every person. For some it may come when they have accomplished something while for others, they may find happiness and a sense of satisfaction when they look back at what they have achieved so far. Happiness is a very personal thing and it varies from person to person. It depends on what you give importance to—what makes one person happy may be immaterial for another person. So, to know when you feel happiest, you must know yourself. You must know your qualities, emotions and temperament. You must also know what matters to you. What gives you most joy and happiness? Have you noticed those times when you just lose track of time when you are engaged in an activity that you love and enjoy?

Happiness is not just about a feel-good emotion; it is also about self-growth. It is said that you will be the happiest when you do something that will also bring you long-term benefits materially, spiritually and emotionally. Happiness is a journey of self-discovery. Those who have discovered and truly understood themselves are by far happier and more contented in life than those who are finding their way around themselves. The first step towards finding happiness is to look within. Once you look within, the answers will slowly start revealing themselves to you. So, take the first step and begin discovering yourself.

4

Why Do You Care More About Others Than Yourself?

Research has shown that those who care more about others than themselves have a higher state of well-being than those inclined otherwise. It is said that focussing attention on others than yourself may be the key to long-term fulfilment.

What are the reasons behind putting others above you?

There are many reasons why people love to help and put others first. Let us dive in to find out:

It is just part of who you are

Everyone has their own way of helping others, but for some, it is just part of who they are. It comes naturally to them. For such people, they may not know why they do so because they have always been that way. It could be because of their upbringing or something that is innate to them. But no matter what the reason is, if helping others is in your true and intrinsic nature, you should be proud of it. It is nothing to be ashamed of.

You want to make the world a better place

You would rather give than receive because you know that giving will help someone in need and make their life better.

Also, you may want to make the world a better place one good deed at a time by helping others when they need it the most. You must note that this quality of helpfulness and giving is not universal and not ingrained in everyone. There will be those who do not have this quality or do not understand the happiness that you receive when you help others. Such people may try to discourage you from helping others. The best way to deal with such kind of people is to ignore them. As stated before, not everyone has magnanimous qualities that you possess, so it is best to let them go their own way. What is important is the sense of genuine well-being you feel when you help someone. Remember that when such people try to discourage you from following your own path.

You genuinely care about others

You want others to be happy. The desire to make the world a better place is something you care about deeply. You believe that service to the community is a noble pursuit and want to contribute in any way possible. We all have faced challenges in our lives. Life at times can be tough and demanding. There are also those days when we question our own existence and whether our lives have any meaning at all. But when you look at people who face even greater challenges like poverty, disease, abuse, etc., you realise that your problems pale in comparison. It is in moments like these that you realise the need to help others in dire need of assistance.

You see the big picture

You are one of those people who would rather help others than yourself because you see the big picture. You believe in making a significant contribution to the world to make it a better place. You realise that you only have one life and try to make the most out of it.

You are unlike other people who take things for granted and only care about themselves

You have a strong sense of duty towards helping others. You believe in being there for others in their times of need. You value what you have and do not take it for granted as you realise that what you consider to be normal may be luxury for others.

Helping others gives you a sense of purpose in life

You believe that life should have meaning. You are not happy with living a mundane life wherein you just go to work and return home. You do not want to just exist, instead, you want your life to have some value and meaning. Helping others gives you a sense of direction in life. When you do so, it gives you a sense of satisfaction that no amount of professional success can replicate. If you make helping others your mission and purpose in life, you will feel that your life has a new value and meaning. You will feel that you are doing something that is real and that really matters. Once you figure out what you have to offer to the world and make it your life's mission, everything else will fall in place.

Helping others has physiological rewards

Altruism when done with the right spirit can boost self-esteem. It can do so in two ways: Firstly, helping others makes you feel good about yourself and secondly, it builds a sense of connection with others. This sense of connection is especially important when you are feeling down or lonely or having negative thoughts. This is exactly why helping others can be beneficial especially when you are feeling down.

Helping others elevates your mood and reduces stress

When you do something good for others, you get a dopamine rush. Dopamine is the "feel-good" chemical because it is associated with joy. Research has shown that dopamine is also involved in increased motivation. This rush is the same one that you get when eat your favourite food. This rush of happiness acts as a motivator to help others, which in turn makes you feel positive.

You want to run away from your own problems

Helping others is a great way to distract yourself from your own problems and negative self-talk. When you are having a bad day, it may be natural and tempting to curl up in your bed, mope about your problems and do nothing. However, this should not be the reason to go out and help others as it is selfish and not genuine. If you want to help someone out of true and genuine compassion, please do it, but if you want to do so to distract yourself from your own problems, the same should preferably be avoided as it will do more harm than good.

You are feeling guilty for not helping someone in the past

Guilt is one of those emotions that is not spoken about much. This feeling manifests itself when you are aware that you have done something wrong. In this case, you may not have helped someone in the past when they genuinely needed it, leading to them being far worse off. This inaction of yours eats into your conscience. Hence, the next time you see someone in true need of help, you do everything in your power to help them.

Your need to feel useful to others

Altruism is one of the best ways to feel useful and important in life. It gives our lives a true purpose and meaning. It is a universal desire to feel needed. We all want to make a difference to the world no matter how small. And when we help others, we feel that we are making a difference.

However, when you are helping someone, ask yourself the following questions:

- Am I doing it to feel good about myself?
- Do I want some recognition?
- Is there any other reward involved?

True helpers do not have any selfish motive attached to their act. They do not expect anything in return. They do it because it is something that is natural and deeply ingrained in them. They do not need any kind of recognition or praise—such things do not hold value to them. They just do what needs to be done because it is the right thing to do.

While helping others and putting others before yourself is a noble quality, the same should not be overdone. You must know when you must care and help others and when you must not. If you are among those people who is always available to help others, there is a danger that you may be taken for granted, and this is not an ideal situation to be in. You must ensure that people recognise that you are taking out your valuable time to assist them. When you realise that someone is not valuing your contribution, do not be afraid to say no—maybe they do not deserve your time and help. Ascertain and identify those people who are truly in need of help.

Remember that your time and effort is a finite resource and it should be appreciated and valued by those in receipt of them. You should never go out of your way to help those who are not in genuine need of the same. Remember that caring for yourself is equally important. Do not put yourself last in the scheme of things—that is unhealthy. You need to find a proper balance between caring too much and caring too little for your own sanity and well-being. Learn to set proper boundaries. Once you do so, those around you will respect you and value your contribution to their lives. Learn to trust your instincts and learn to walk away from something or someone who is not good for you.

Conclusion

Caring about others is indeed a wonderful quality to have, but this too must be done in moderation. Know when you have nothing more to give, there is nothing wrong in that. It is only when you are satisfied and content with yourself that you can help others. Build yourself up so that you have enough and adequate reserves of energy and compassion that you can be there for others when they truly and genuinely need it. This requires practice and a great degree of self-awareness and does not come overnight.

5

How To Start Loving Yourself

What is self-love? It means that you have an appreciation and positive regard for yourself. It is closely related to self-esteem and self-compassion. You treat yourself in a loving way and understand your own value when you have a strong sense of self-love. Unlike narcissism, which involves excessive self-absorption and self-interest, self-love is a positive trait.

Loving yourself means having a good understanding of both your strengths and weaknesses. A high level of self-love has a positive impact on your well-being, mental fitness and relationships. While you may have been told that "you cannot expect anyone to love you until you love yourself", for those people who have a traumatic past or are in a difficult relationships or any number of other painful experiences, self-love may not be as easy as it sounds. But the important thing is that *self-love is a skill that you can develop*—much like self-confidence and self-trust.

Why is self-love important?

Self-love is critical to our overall well-being. And loving yourself does not mean that you do not hold yourself to a high standard. Self-love does not mean that you allow yourself to be lazy or below par in your day-to-day work. On the contrary, without feeling positively towards yourself, you may find it hard to be motivated. Many studies have shown that you need self-love in order to take action, take chances and welcome opportunities with confidence and composure. Self-love will empower you to take risks and to say no to things that do not work for you. It is a key component of building self-compassion. Self-love helps you to take care of yourself, strive for success and lower stress. It also acts as a shield against negative thinking and emotions and self-sabotage. It also helps you to say "no" and guides you so that you do not push yourself too far.

Self-love is rooted in science. There are several benefits of having a high degree of self-love. So, let us delve deeper and unpack the layers.

Lowers stress, builds higher resilience

Experiencing stress is uncomfortable and when under strain, challenges may seem insurmountable to you. Your will to tackle them may suffer and you may feel bogged down. Negative feelings and self-critical thoughts usually accompany stress making you feel even more dejected. However, when you have a strong sense of self-love, you will find it easier to tackle stress. That being said, it must be noted that stress does not discriminate—people with a high level of self-love also experience stress. But what sets them apart from others is that they are able to deal with it in a more mature and better way. You will agree that when you feel good, it will be easier to solve the problem. Self-love and self-compassion are directly linked. *When you have a high degree of self-love, you will look at challenges as opportunities to grow.* While setbacks will affect you, their effects will be temporary and will not dent your spirits. Self-compassion and, by extension, self-love, not only help you bounce back, but also aid in keeping you mentally fit.

Increases willingness to take risks

You can take risks only when you have a great degree of faith in yourself. And having self-love ensures that you have the appropriate mindset to take on risks and challenges head-on with full confidence and faith in yourself. You know that you will be able to handle and deal with the outcome or result of your actions even if it is not what you want. You will look at a setback as a learning experience and not a failure and will not lose your confidence in yourself. You will also believe that the time and effort is worth the investment. When you love yourself, you will be able to correctly identify opportunities for growth thereby allowing you to prosper. Risk-taking is not mindless and does not involve doing something that seems fun. You realise that staying in your comfort zone ensures stagnation, not growth. Growth comes from stepping out of your comfort zone and taking risks. With a high degree of self-love, you will be able to give yourself the best chance of succeeding.

Develops empathy

It is only when we accept ourselves with our various strengths and weaknesses with the required compassion and appreciation, that we can have compassion for others. Having empathy ensures that you have a deeper level of connection with people thereby creating a sense of belonging.

Builds self-efficacy

Self-efficacy encompasses a person's confidence in themselves to control their behaviour and stay motivated in pursuit of their goals. To ascertain whether you have self-efficacy, you must ask yourself the question: When facing a challenge, do you feel that you can rise up and accomplish your goal or do you accept defeat? The most important component of self-efficacy is feeling good about yourself and your abilities. When your self-confidence is high, you are able to take on new challenges with self-assurance and faith in yourself. This will help you to achieve your goals and live your best life.

Ways to practise self-love

There are many ways to achieve self-love. A few are discussed here.

Understand that sometimes societal expectations offer unrealistic standards

You are unique. There is nobody else like you. Hence, you should ideally not be compared to anyone else. You are the only one you should compare yourself to. Human beings constantly want more and more. Hence, even if you do achieve a huge milestone, your mind will not be satisfied and will always crave more. So, avoid comparing yourself with that unattainable ideal as doing so will only make you feel bad for yourself.

Live in the moment

While this is ideal, it is easier said than done. The human mind is functioned and designed to constantly shift between anxieties of the past and worries about the future. It is very rarely, if ever, focussed on the present time and moment. But still, try to live in the moment even if it is for a short period of time. Try to let go of your worries and anxieties for those moments and embrace life. In this moment, realise how fortunate you are to be a living, breathing and functioning human being.

Practise gratitude

Practising gratitude is the key to happiness and loving yourself. You can do so by starting a gratitude journal wherein you take out as little as five minutes daily to think about things that you are thankful for in your life—your home, your family, your health, your country, your life and so on. Once you show gratitude on a regular basis, you will realise its benefits such as improvement in your overall well-being.

Embrace the fact that you cannot control everything

You must accept that everything is not in your control. There are things which are outside your sphere of influence such as the weather, other people, their decisions and actions. What is in your control is your actions and reactions to the events around you. So, instead of trying to control everything in your life, try to focus on how you respond to it. Do the best you can do and then learn to let go and accept that it is no longer in your hands and let things work themselves out. Slowly but surely, everything will resolve itself.

Self-care

While there may be those who may want to impress upon you that self-care is selfish, know that they are not right. Self-care is an intrinsic part of a person's well-being and should not be ignored. Self-care is one of the best ways to practice self-love.

Eat healthy

What you eat affects not only your body, but also your mind. If you eat something heavy and oily, it impacts you physically but at the same time your mind will also feel lethargic. So, eat foods that impact your body and mind in a positive way.

Get moving

A good workout is important for physical and mental well-being. Research has shown that having regular workouts ensures that feel-good chemicals are secreted in your brain which give you a sense of well-being. You do not need to join a gym or workout class as workouts can be done at home itself. Learn to make your workouts a priority and soon you will realise its huge benefits.

Be unique

Take pride in your uniqueness. Be happy that there is something that sets you apart from others.

Let go of toxic relationships

Not all relationships are beneficial to you. There are those that do you more harm than good. Once you identify these toxic relationships, and realise that being in contact with such people is not helping you in any way, learn to let go of them. Such people do not deserve to be a part of your life.

Meditate

Take out a few minutes every day to meditate. Breathe in and out and let go of all the negativity in your life. You can also include self-reflection in your routine along with meditation.

List positive things about yourself

Make a list of your best traits and accomplishments the next time you feel joyous and in control of your life. While it might sound a little cheesy, it can be a great reminder when you are having a less-than-stellar day. Although it may be challenging initially, developing this habit can help you learn to accept yourself.

Stop being too tough on yourself

While you may love being your biggest critic, try to be kind to yourself now and then. One of the biggest things that may prevent you from engaging in true self-love is being too tough on yourself.

Manage stress

Stress prevention is a huge need in this day and age and can help in managing health conditions like possible heart disease, high blood pressure and depression.

Treat others with love and respect

While everyone may not return the favour, learn to always treat others with love and respect. In short, treat them the way you would like to be treated.

Celebrate milestones

Celebrate your milestones and victories whether they are big or small. Learn to pat yourself on the back and be happy with your accomplishments. Celebrating your achievements helps you build self-esteem and stay motivated in life.

Give up the need for approval from others

Realise that you do not need approval from others to love yourself. If you have a high degree of self-confidence and self-worth, you will realise that what others think does not matter that much to you. Learn to trust yourself and your intuition. This will help you in the long run.

Be realistic

Nobody on this planet experiences happiness every second of every day. Do you understand the reason? After all, we are all human. We all make errors and have mixed emotions, and that is okay. *Embrace your humanity.* You can develop a realistic mentality by practising it. We are often overly hard on ourselves, so learning to be realistic will aid you in your quest for self-love.

So, to conclude, self-love is something that can be cultivated and built over time. It requires adequate time, effort and consistency. But once you know how to do so, you will surely reap the rewards of this wonderful feeling.

6

How To Put Your Needs Above Anyone Else's

The one thing that schools should teach is the importance of putting yourself first. It is difficult to do so in a culture that valorises prioritising others, and in a day and age when social media is abuzz with examples that glorify and glamorise putting others above yourself. One of the first things you need to understand is that putting yourself first does not mean you are selfish instead, it means that you have a high degree of self-care and self-awareness, qualities rarely found in people. Selfish people think only about themselves without any regard or care for others around them. Putting yourself first involves taking care of your own needs, requirements and feelings as well as of others, but doing so in a way that is best for you and does not cause any harm or damage to someone else. And doing this is extremely important because nobody else will do it for you. You have the sole responsibility for maintaining your own mental and physical health. Building and nurturing the life you want and desire is your responsibility. In order to get what you need and desire, you have to ask for it and work towards it because no one else is going to do that for you.

Effects of lack of self-care

As mentioned before, having a high degree of self-care is extremely important for everyone. When practised properly, it can lead to a longer, happier and healthier life. There are several risk factors which come into play when one does not practise the required degree of self-care. Let us delve deeper into this.

Changes in sleep patterns

One of the effects of having a lower degree of self-care is manifested in changes in your sleep patterns. *Sleep is a necessity and not a luxury.* Yes, there are those who glorify *hustle culture* which involves being on the job at ungodly hours and having just bare minimum sleep. But this habit is harmful in the long run and will lead to major health problems. Research has shown that humans require anything between six to eight hours of uninterrupted sleep to function at optimum levels. You will notice that if you do not sleep well for even one night, it will have a negative effect on you the next day leading to you feeling groggy, irritable and lacking the required focus and attention to get your tasks done. If you are finding it difficult to sleep when experiencing stress, you can listen to relaxing music or have a long, leisurely hot bath to induce a sense of calmness before you go to bed.

Changes in appetite

Another side effect of a lack of adequate self-care is unusual changes in appetite. Your appetite may either increase or decrease leading you to having unhealthy fluctuations in weight. Stress can disrupt hunger cues leading you to either not eat much or eat too much. You may have the sudden urge to indulge in something sugary, fried or oily and rich to curb the uncomfortable feeling you are experiencing. Indulging in comfort food when stressed is called "stress eating" and is not a healthy occurrence. So, monitor your normal hunger patterns and look out for unusual fluctuations in appetite and cravings.

Emotional outbursts

You must observe your normal and natural mood and mindset. When you do so, you will be able to identify behavioural patterns which are out of the ordinary for you. For example, if you are constantly irritated, unable to control your anger, have outbursts of emotions or are distressed about things or events which usually would not bother you much, something is amiss. Mood swings and emotional outbursts typically indicate a presence of high level of stress, anxiety or fatigue among other things and is a sign that you need to take better care of yourself. Such mood swings can have an adverse impact on your work, social and daily life as well.

Feeling uninterested

Do you feel like you don't want to do anything and just want to lie in bed all day and watch your favourite sitcom? If this is happening on a regular basis, and is impacting your work and daily chores, it is time to introspect. Take time out to analyse why you are feeling so. What triggered it initially? What is exacerbating it now? Once you identify the root cause, take the required adequate steps to ensure that you get back to your normal self.

Difficulty in taking decisions

When under an unusual or high degree of stress, you will experience difficulty in taking even mundane decisions. When you are your normal self, you won't think twice before taking these decisions, but now that you are under strain, it will stump you and result in you feeling indecisive.

Feelings of worthlessness

There is nothing wrong in being self-critical. This ensures that you push yourself to the desired limit to achieve your current goal. However, when feelings of low self-esteem or worthlessness start swirling in your mind, it can be debilitating. Learn to monitor your thoughts and ascertain when negative self-talk becomes prominent in your mind. When that begins to dominate, you should realise that you need to take remedial action. Having feelings of inadequacy or worthlessness, if unchecked, can lead to depression. This in turn will negatively affect your social and professional life.

Frequently falling sick

Unhealthy emotions like excessive stress and lack of self-worth can have worrying physical manifestations. You may be falling sick with alarming regularity leading to loss of productivity. Here, it is important to have a high degree of self-awareness so that you understand when your body is not feeling like it normally does. When you realise this, you can take the required steps and necessary help from professionals to ensure that you get back to your energetic normal self.

How to put yourself first

There is a famous saying: *You can't pour from an empty cup*. This is directly linked to self-care, meaning that if you do not take care of yourself, how can you be expected to take care of others? So, let us discuss how you can start putting yourself first:

Set personal boundaries

While it is fashionable to be a "yes" man (or woman), doing so can actually be detrimental to you. If you are not careful, people will demand too much of you and at times also take you for granted. To prevent this, learn to establish boundaries with your family, friends and co-workers so that you can put yourself first when necessary. However, this does not mean that you should not be a helpful and supportive person. It means that you should be there for others but only when it does not affect you negatively or impact your important and critical tasks. Never go out of your way to help anyone unnecessarily. Do so only if it is someone you know who genuinely needs it. When your boundaries are encroached upon, learn to tell the person that the same is not appreciated. This requires practice and at times can lead to unpleasant situations. But if done respectfully and assertively, it can lead to improvement in your mental health and overall well-being.

Ask for help when you need it

You cannot do everything on your own. If you feel that you are swamped with work or commitments, learn to accept that it is fine to delegate or request someone else to do the work if and when possible. Everyone needs a helping hand from time to time and there is no shame in asking for assistance, guidance or support.

Prioritise rest

As mentioned before, rest and sleep are requirements and not luxuries. There will be times when you may have to rest even when tasks are incomplete. There is absolutely no shame in this. You must realise that you have to fill your cup first before filling someone else's. Make sure that you take adequate rest during the week, treating it like a critical task and sticking to it. It can be for a few minutes or few hours, but learn that it is extremely important for your physical and mental well-being.

Reduce stress

Do not allow stress to build up to an unhealthy level. Learn to incorporate stress relievers in your daily habits. You can do so by savouring hot, herbal tea, lighting a candle and listening to calming music, taking a bath with scented bath salts or going for a leisurely walk in the outdoors.

Take out some time every day for a fun activity

Having fun is of vital importance as embodied by the adage *all work and no play makes Jack a dull boy*. Make sure that you indulge in some enjoyable fun activity like watching your favourite TV show, reading, working on a puzzle or playing a game with your loved ones. This will ensure that you get refreshed.

Develop a hobby

Pick up an old hobby or develop a new one that brings you joy. Having a hobby ensures that you lighten up your day. You engage in your hobby because it brings you fun and joy. Engage in your hobby at least once a week, even if it is for a few minutes.

Practise gratitude

Cultivate an attitude of thankfulness and gratitude. When practised regularly, you will feel happier, calm and more fulfilled. To do so, focus on the good things in your life and make a gratitude list wherein you mention three things that you are grateful for every day.

Eat a healthy, balanced diet

Having a healthy, balanced and nutritious diet gives you energy and supports good health. In general, eat more fruits, vegetables and complex carbs while limiting your salt, fat and sugar intake. To ensure that you eat healthy, you can do meal prep on Sundays where you plan for the meals you will eat in the coming week.

Exercise regularly

We need to take care of our bodies. After all, it is the only one we have. Regular exercise and workouts not only improve your physical health, but also ensure that you feel mentally fresh. Exercise increases blood flow to the muscles and the brain leading to a feeling of general well-being. Do any kind of exercise which you find enjoyable whether it be the gym, free-hand workouts or even walking.

Try meditation

Regular meditation reduces stress levels, improves concentration and ensures an overall sense of well-being. It can be done for as little as ten or fifteen minutes a day. When you incorporate this in your daily routine, you will reap amazing benefits.

Treat yourself with compassion

You are only human, and it is natural that once in a while you will make mistakes. In these moments, remember to be kind to yourself. If you are too hard on yourself, there are chances that you may get burnt out. When you do something wrong, acknowledge your responsibility and try to make it right. Learn and analyse as to what went wrong so that the next time you do not make the same mistake.

Trust yourself

You must be your own biggest supporter. Listen to your inner voice when making decisions. After all, you know yourself better than anyone else. Start surrounding yourself with people who genuinely and truly support you. Such people will be kind to you while at the same time not shy away from giving constructive criticism. Also, learn to speak kindly to yourself.

Engaging in meaningful self-care requires consistent practice and is developed over a period of time. That being said, if you do not know where or how to begin, you can consult a mental health professional to guide you in your quest. These professionals have gone through the required theoretical and practical training ensuring that they have the required skills and know-how to make you the best you can be.

7
How To Stop Caring About What Others Think Of You

Humans are social animals. We live and function in groups. Hence, it is natural that we will think and to a large extent also care what others think of us. We would like to be liked and accepted by our peer group and also build bonds of friendship and companionship with them. It is said that caring about what others think of us is a survival mechanism as old as humanity itself. It is definitely healthy to align yourself with the social order and behave, at least publicly, according to generally accepted norms and standards, thereby building sustainable and solid relationships.

But that said, there does come a point when caring about what others think becomes unhealthy. We must ensure that in the race to being socially accepted, we do not let go of our core intrinsic values, traits and principles.

Signs of an approval addict

We must be careful and ensure that our "need" for approval does not get out of control, thus making us an "approval addict". To know more about this, let us delve into what it means to be an "approval addict" so that you can take remedial action in case you exhibit one or more of the signs. Being an approval addict can negatively impact your mental health and relationships. In this state, your primary motivator is others liking you and approving of you. If you are an approval addict, you will base your self-worth on what others think of you and not on your own core sense of self. Your moods and state of mind will fluctuate according to the perception the public holds about you. You will worry excessively about what others think of you and whether you have done anything to upset them. This can often lead you to feeling low, confused, insecure, lonely and anxious.

So, what are the signs of an approval addict?

You struggle to form your own opinions

When asked for your opinion, you often freeze up or choose to ignore what you truly believe and instead go with what your peer group is thinking. You will do anything to avoid risking upsetting or offending others. You will be so focussed on pleasing others that you will not even know what you think. Instead of looking inwards and trying to ascertain what you think of a particular subject, you look outwards and align your thinking with the people surrounding you and say what you have to in order to be liked and accepted.

You have trouble saying no

When you are an approval addict, saying no to someone is terrifying. You find it easier to say yes and go along with the flow despite the inconvenience it causes you because your focus is on pleasing others.

You go along to get along

Addiction to approval can lead you to going along with what others say even if it does not work for you. This is a very worrying habit as it can lead to you being in potentially unpleasant, risky or even dangerous circumstances.

You apologise too much

There is nothing wrong in apologising if you do something wrong. But when you are an approval addict, you will apologise even when you have done nothing wrong.

You have low self-esteem

Approval addicts get their esteem from the approval of others. Their entire locus of thought is directed towards what others think of them and not on what they think of themselves. Approval addicts often lack self-worth, thus leading to low self-esteem. When others get upset or angry at such people, they are devastated because they feel that their value is at risk.

You constantly put others' needs above your own

The most important thing to approval addicts is keeping those around them happy. Their own happiness is not important to them. They will ignore or minimise their own needs to ensure that people are happy and don't think of them negatively.

You feel anxious about what others think of you

An approval addict will constantly obsess over how others perceive them. It must be kept in mind that if this obsession becomes too severe, it may result in anxiety disorders or OCD.

You try to present yourself in the best possible light

When you are an approval addict, you only reveal those parts of yourself that make you viewed upon positively. Additionally, you actively try to suppress that side of you which you believe will be looked upon negatively.

You are terrified of rejection

Getting rejected is one of the scariest things for an approval addict. Dealing with rejection is difficult for everyone, but it is especially more challenging for approval addicts.

How to stop being an approval addict

So, now that we know what it means to be addicted to approval, let us look into the ways in which we stop being overtly affected by what others think of us.

Identify your values

What are your values? They are the "why" behind everything you do. Everyone has different values, and unless they are dangerous or antisocial, they should be nurtured and valued. To begin with, list five values in your life. This list can be a gauge to evaluate your life decisions rather than making choices that you think your social group will approve of. When you live your life according to your own intrinsic values, you will slowly learn to love and respect yourself, and gradually, your need to please others will dissipate.

Pick and choose the people you share space with

Surround yourself with people who truly care about you. Every person who spends time with you is not your well-wisher. There may be those who are just around you because they have nothing better to do. There are also those who secretly harbour ill-will against you. Identify such insincere people and learn to distance yourself from them. People who truly care about you will support you but at the same time will not be averse to giving you constructive criticism. Learn to distinguish between genuine criticism and the kind of criticism which finds its roots in envy and ill-will. Once you do so and you identify the circle of people you want to be with, your life will be richer and more valuable.

Distance yourself from toxic people

As mentioned in the previous section, not everyone is your well-wisher. Additionally, there are those people whose presence in your life causes you only pain and discomfort. You do not benefit from your association with such people. Learn to accept that it is better to have a few genuine friends who truly care about you rather than surrounding yourself with a huge number of people just to make up the numbers.

Take a social media break

Social media is both a boon and a bane. While the world has become more connected than ever with the advent of apps like X, Facebook and Instagram, too much of it is detrimental to your well-being. Plus, scrolling through the content on social media is addictive and takes up loads of your time without you even realising it. It also leads to attention disorders and lack of focus. So, identify when social media becomes too much for you to handle and take a break when required. It must be noted that many a time social media can become excessively toxic and abusive especially when the discussion veers towards controversial subjects like politics, religion or history. We can do without this unnecessary conflict which do not add any meaningful value in our lives. The only thing this kind of discourse brings out is negativity and toxicity and it is best we distance ourselves from this. If you have people on your social media who constantly post such negative, abusive and upsetting content, you can stop following them. By doing so, you have not only disconnected with the person digitally, but also distanced yourself from their opinions which cause you nothing but anguish.

Accept that you cannot please everyone

You must accept that everyone has their own set of beliefs and values. It may be hard to believe, but some people like to be angry and upset because they believe it keeps them on their toes. In this regard, remember that you cannot please everyone. And honestly, it is not worth it to please everyone, especially if it is causing your mental health to suffer.

Let it go

Fortunately or unfortunately, you cannot control what and how other people think. Everyone has their own reasoning for the way they think and function and they believe that they are right in their own way. For many, their core beliefs or values are things that are formed after several years and will not change irrespective of what facts and figures you place in front of them. You must accept that you cannot argue with someone who does not want to understand. They are built in their own ways, whether for good or bad, and will not change irrespective of what happens. Learn to accept them as they are and let it slide. In short, learn to let go.

Do not compare yourself to others and despair

Everyone is unique. Even though two people may be of similar age, they have different upbringing and journeys. What they value and pay attention to also differs widely. One person may have excelled in his academic career while another has done well in extracurricular activities. We are all in different phases of our journeys and to be honest, comparing oneself to others will only bring about envy and discontent. It is best that we do without these negative emotions. Our life is challenging enough as is and the presence of these unproductive thoughts does not help us in anyway. So, slowly and gradually make a conscious effort to stop comparing yourself with others.

Forgive yourself

Everyone makes mistakes at certain points in time. After all, we are human. Instead of worrying about what others will think about you when you have made the mistake, try to forgive yourself and attempt to learn where you went wrong so that when you are in a similar situation in the future, you do not make the same mistake.

Try affirmations

Inculcate a habit of positive self-talk. This habit will reap immense benefits for you. When you speak to yourself in a positive way and reassure yourself that things will work out for you, you slowly begin to believe in it. You will believe that things will start going well for you and before you know it, you will actually experience success.

How to value yourself

Finally, let us look at ways in which you can start valuing yourself. This is a critical quality required to lead a happy and fulfilling life.

Be grateful for your effort

Pat yourself on the back when you are struggling or having a horrid day but still put in the required effort. Just getting out of bed and turning up on those days when you are suffering and under duress is one of the most difficult things to do. Appreciate yourself for putting in the effort when you didn't have the mind or inclination to do it.

Do not settle for less

We all deserve to be happy in life. If you realise that you are unhappy, identify the source of your unhappiness and ask yourself what will make you happy. You do not have to tolerate anyone or anything that causes pain or suffering. While we may often think that we have to sacrifice our own happiness in order to achieve something, it is not entirely true. There are always choices in life. Learn to choose the path that makes you feel satisfied.

When in doubt, remember your perseverance

Life can be tough and challenging. It also throws us new challenges constantly which may make us question our own abilities. In such times, when you are doubting yourself, remember the instances in your past when you faced a challenge but did not back off. Remember when you faced the challenge head-on and emerged victorious. Reliving your previous success stories will improve your self-confidence and will give you the required composure and assurance that you can handle any challenge that is thrown your way.

While developing a considerable sense of self-worth may seem daunting, complex and time-consuming, do not be afraid as this is a common misconception. All you have to do to develop self-worth is take small and gradual steps to create a gentle shift in perspective on how you show up in life. These small but critical steps will make all the difference in the long run and will benefit you immensely.

8

Who Are You Now?

All of us have faced challenges and reached where we are today. As we learnt, we also grew along the way. We learnt new skills, sharpened old ones and made us better versions of ourselves. This, in short, is called self-growth.

So, what is self-growth? Self-growth is defined as an intrinsic process in which you develop and expand your abilities. Self-growth has various, far-reaching effects which can lead to your growth in all aspects—personal, professional and spiritual. It can help you achieve your full potential. Self-growth results in an increase in personal resources such as self-esteem and coping skills as well as changes in your philosophy towards life and can include a deeper sense of spirituality, redefined priorities and an overall greater appreciation for life.

Self-growth and its importance

Self-growth can manifest in varied ways in different people, such as:

- Learning to have a better control on your emotions.
- Developing a growth mindset.
- Learning to be more resilient.
- Accepting what you can and cannot change.
- Knowing and understanding yourself.

- Beating procrastination.
- Improving your emotional intelligence.

So, why is self-growth important? We all know that life is a continuous learning process. Therefore, it is imperative that you continue developing and working on yourself if you want to grow and experience more of life. Otherwise, life can feel stagnant if you keep on doing the same things over and over again, without adding value to yourself. Self-growth involves self-development which means taking the necessary steps to make positive changes in your life. Along the way, you will create new goals that will only benefit you once you develop yourself. Also, there are several benefits to self-growth:

You gain a greater awareness of yourself

Let me ask you a question. How well do you know yourself? It is a question that is not easy to answer, right? However, once you start engaging in self-development and self-growth, you will start learning more about yourself. You will gain a greater sense of self-awareness. Self-development requires knowing your abilities, values, characteristics, weaknesses and strengths. This process is necessary to know what direction you want to go in life.

Your confidence level will rise

Greater self-awareness helps in boosting your self-confidence levels. Once you have greater self-assurance, you will gain new knowledge, learn new techniques and will be able to overcome challenges that you earlier found difficult to handle or surmount. Additionally, constant improvement and success can boost morale, leading to higher self-esteem and confidence. Finally, self-growth drives motivation, which pushes you to scale new peaks and brave new horizons, which you may not have thought were possible earlier.

You can aim for new goals in life

There is more to life than having a stable job and being able to buy things you want. You must realise that knowing yourself well can be instrumental in opening up new paths and finding new opportunities. Now may be the right time to follow your childhood passion. Do what you can to make yourself happy and fulfilled based on your existing skill levels while learning new ones along the way.

You become more open-minded

When you constantly incorporate learning and development in your life, you become exposed to various ideas and thoughts that can open up opportunities in various avenues of your life. Continuous learning and growth make you view life with a fresh and new perspective thereby broadening your horizons. It encourages you to step out of your comfort zone, thereby expanding your perspective and making you want to try new ways of doing things. Open-mindedness makes you shake your limiting beliefs and helps you attain a growth-oriented mindset that will assist in your overall personal development.

You get to figure out where to take your life

There is no template or set pattern to live your life. Just because a majority of people are happy completing their education, landing a job and getting married, does not mean that you should go with the flow. There isn't a universal direction for everyone to take. Do not be afraid to forge your own path. That said, gaining an education is a must and definitely a non-negotiable. Work on getting to know yourself better so that you can unlock your personal vision on what you want to accomplish in life. When you know where you are going, it is easy to be motivated, and it is easier to lead a fulfilling life.

You will get closer to success

When you start working on your life, getting to know yourself and acquiring new skills along the way, you just take a step closer to success. While success means different things to different people, it almost always involves incredible level of hard work, dedication and commitment. All of this starts with you knowing yourself better and committing to your goals. Success will only come closer as you start living a more fulfilling and meaningful life.

Tips for self-growth

So, now that we know why self-growth is important, let us go through some great self-improvement.

Read every day

Books are incredible sources of wisdom and knowledge. The more books you read the wiser you will become. Making reading a habit is an indispensable ingredient to sustained and consistent self-growth.

Learn a new language

Learning a new language is a challenge for your brain and leads to increase in knowledge and self-growth. However, while selecting a language to learn, do keep in mind as to whether it will help you in your life in the future as well. For example, one of the most widely spoken languages in the world is Spanish as it is spoken not only in Spain, but also in most countries of South and Central America. Learning a language like Spanish can not only lead to personal growth but can also open up new doors for you professionally.

Overcome your fears

Whether it be a fear of public speaking, uncertainty or even something like heights, fear is something that holds you back and prevents you from improving and growing. Identify the fears that you want to work on so that you can grow and prosper in life.

Wake up early

Waking up early has been acknowledged as a habit that improves productivity. When you wake up in the early hours of the morning, you have several hours to incorporate healthy and mindful habits in your daily routine. It also ensures that you are mentally ready to take on the day. By waking up early, you can enjoy the tranquillity of dawn when the normal hustle-bustle is absent and you can also absorb the first rays of sunshine which help your brain switch on into active mode.

Start your life handbook

A life handbook is a book that contains the essentials on how you can live your life to the fullest, such as your purpose, your values and your goals. It can be thought of as a manual for how to live your best life through consistent self-improvement.

Write a letter to your future self

Where do you see yourself five or ten years down the future? What kind of person will you be after you have had years and years of self-improvement under your belt? Write a letter to your future self and seal it. Then start working towards being the person you want to open the letter.

Get out of your comfort zone

Real growth comes with hard work and sweat and almost exclusively happens outside of your comfort zone. It is called comfort zone for a reason—when you are comfortable, you are satiated and satisfied and have no need to work on anything or improve. Being in the comfort zone for too long leads to stagnation. So, begin by identifying where your comfort zone lines are and how you can begin to step out of them little by little.

Stay focussed on to-do lists

Having a to-do list ensures that your life has a certain structure. You know what you need to do during the day, what activities are critical and which are not so important. Without a to-do list, your day can potentially become unstructured and chaotic. Maintaining this list also safeguards you against forgetting any task.

Acknowledge your flaws

As human beings, we all have flaws. But it is important to acknowledge, identify and work on them to ensure that they do not create a barrier between you and your goals. However, when thinking of your flaws, remember to do so with a sense of self-love. Do not look at them in a critical or negative way. This exercise is about finding areas you can improve upon and not about finding things that are wrong with you.

Get into action

No amount of theory can teach you what actually doing something can. Therefore, get up from your comfortable couch and start taking decisive and constructive action. Identify something that you have been meaning to do and start working on it immediately.

Learn from people who inspire you

Think about the people who inspire you. Read about them, their journey and how they reached the heights that they have. Reflect on their qualities and identify which of those qualities you would want to incorporate in your own personality. However, while doing so, remember not to copy someone else. While it is perfectly alright to admire and aspire to be like someone else, you must never lose sight of your true inherent personality. Your personality is something that is unique and should be cherished and celebrated. So, incorporate some of their qualities, but do so mindfully.

Quit a bad habit

Ask yourself if you have any bad habit that you need to eliminate. This can include oversleeping, smoking, drinking or procrastinating. However, while attempting to quit your unhealthy habit, remember to do so in a mindful way so that the change is permanent and not temporary. Many a time, many people quit a bad habit only to go back to it during times of stress and strain. Keep in mind that while it is difficult to quit a bad habit, reacquiring it does not take much time. So, ensure that you are aware of the triggers that push you into the pattern of bad habits so that you can work on them holistically and constructively.

Avoid negative people

Wherever you go, there are bound to be negative people. If you cannot avoid them indefinitely, try to limit the time you spend with them to avoid feeling bogged down by them.

Learn to deal with difficult people

There are certain situations where you cannot avoid difficult people. For example, if these people are your colleagues or your close relatives, avoiding them will not be possible. In such scenarios, learn to deal with them in a constructive manner that leads to maintenance of cordial relations. While dealing with such people, application of people-management skills comes in handy.

Reduce the time you spend on social media

Social media use, if unchecked, can lead to wastage of valuable time that could otherwise be spent doing productive work. Keep a track of the time you spend on these apps and if possible, put limits on them.

Learn chess

Chess is a terrific game to learn strategy and improve your brain power. It is a wonderful way to have fun and it also makes you exercise your analytical skills.

Reduce the time you spend watching TV

Be mindful of the amount of time you spend watching TV. While there are many programmes which increase your knowledge, there are also those which solely serve to entertain and distract. Learn to monitor the amount of time you spend in front of your television as the same time could be productively used elsewhere, such as with close friends, engaging in a hobby or exercising.

Start a thirty-day challenge

Set a goal and give yourself thirty days to achieve it. Your goal could be anything from sticking with a new habit to developing a new hobby. Thirty days is enough time to plan, strategize, review and engage yourself in action which will propel you towards your goal.

Meditate

Meditation when done correctly helps to calm you, improves your concentration levels and enables you to be more conscious while at the same time improving your overall mental health. Meditation can also help you sleep better, be more active and productive, and be kinder to people around you.

Learn public speaking

Public speaking is one of the most common fears that people have. Public speaking can help you to communicate better, present yourself and engage with people. This skill will help you both personally and professionally and will reap dividends for you as you will be able to perform better in meetings and presentations.

Network with experts

Connect and interact with experts who have great accomplishments in their respective fields. Such people have done so with the right skill set, attitude and know-how. Learn from them as to how they overcame the various challenges that they had to encounter along the way. By gaining these valuable insights, you can improve your own self and attempt to achieve similar results in your life.

Let go of the past

Holding on to grievances or unhappiness stemming from past experiences will only be detrimental to your mental health and overall well-being. Ruminating over such occurrences only harms you and prevents you from moving on and becoming a better person. Learn to break away from the past, forgive yourself and move on in life.

You have reached so far in life by overcoming various challenges and obstacles. But remember that self-growth is a constant and continuous process. It never truly stops. While being satisfied with what you have achieved thus far, remember that you still have a long way to go. This is a lifelong commitment and one that reaps tremendous benefits. The results may not always be immediate, but if you stick with it, they will surely come and you will definitely see a positive change in yourself and your life.

9
How Can You Stop Feeling Bad For Yourself

Sometimes life ca be tough, and we may face problems which at times seem insurmountable. There may also be those occasions when we have worked hard and diligently towards achieving a goal but ended up failing or experiencing rejection. It is part and parcel of life to feel sorry for ourselves every once in a while, when we are facing such challenging moments or situations. Everyone has felt self-pity at a certain point in their life.

Self-pity and its signs

In fact, self-pity is an important emotion which compels us to focus on and process something we are struggling with or finding stressful or disappointing such as missing out on a promotion at work which you think you deserved, failing an exam for which you had studied diligently, grappling with a long-term friendship that is disintegrating or dealing with financial woes. While this self-directed sadness may initially and briefly hinder us from doing what we do best, we need to take this time to consider our options, devise a strategy for the future and then move forward with renewed clarity.

So, self-pity is one of the natural emotions that we experience in response to certain harrowing events in our lives. While it can be soothing, thereby giving us time to work out what we need to do next, self-pity is never the solution to any problem.

We must be mindful that we do not make self-pity our regular state of mind. Being preoccupied with our thoughts and always having thoughts like "why is this happening with me only?" or "why don't things go my way" is not healthy. If unchecked and not worked upon, your mindset can get stuck and it may lead to anxiety, depression and feelings of isolation.

If we stay in a state of self-pity for too long, it can be unproductive and act as a hindrance to us living life to the fullest and functioning at our optimum levels. If someone is stuck in this state, it can rob them of achieving anything meaningful in their lives. Such people struggle to do anything productive, lose track of their goals and in general are not happy. Self-pity can, if noticed by others, be a way of receiving helpful advice which can be instrumental in working out of that phase. However, if someone is full of self-pity too frequently and for too long, that person can be viewed by others as someone who focuses excessively on the negatives, complains too much, is petulant and someone who should be avoided.

While self-pity is not an official mental health diagnosis, it is clear that too much self-pity is extremely detrimental to living a healthy and fulfilling life. There are also high chances that someone stuck in self-pity may look to numb their feelings by turning to alcohol, drugs or certain unhealthy behaviours.

In order to stop feeling sorry for yourself, you first need to analyse why you are feeling this way. Self-pity is a sign that you are still holding on to a past trauma or loss. You may unknowingly be engaging in self-pity if you do not know the signs and symptoms of it, which are:

Feeling like a victim

You constantly feel that you are wronged. It may feel that the world is conspiring against you. Questions like "why me?" or "why is this happening with me?" keep swirling in your mind.

Believing that no one else can understand your situation

You may believe that you are the only one suffering and that everyone is happy and satisfied with their life. This is not true. Everyone has their own varied challenges in life. Everyone faces multiple issues which cause them stress and discomfort. Remember that you are not alone. Don't be afraid to ask for help from someone who you truly trust.

Blaming others for your mistakes

The responsibility for your mistakes lies with you and you alone. Deflecting the blame towards others is unproductive and lacks meaning. Learn to take responsibility for the mistakes which have taken place on your watch and be accountable for them.

Feeling like you are entitled to special treatment

This is something that one should ideally refrain from. As mentioned before, everyone has their own issues and challenges in life. One should learn how to navigate through them without complaining. The notion that one is entitled to special treatment is incorrect on multiple levels and is an idea that should not be entertained.

Feeling like you are not good enough

Feelings of inadequacy usually accompany self-pity. Such feelings should be worked through so that they don't result in further complications.

Here is why self-pity should be avoided

So, now that we have understood what self-pity is and how it affects your life, it is time to take action and stop feeling sorry for yourself. Here are some of the reasons why you should make this change.

It is a waste of time and energy

Self-pity can be emotionally draining and can sap your energy and motivation. The time spent in feeling sorry for yourself can instead be invested in doing something that can help you feel more positive about yourself.

You are only hurting yourself

Self-pity if unchecked can lead to self-destructive behaviour like excessive drinking or engaging in risky activities. These behaviours have long-term negative consequences. So, it is important to take constructive action and work on yourself to ensure that you grow emotionally, professionally and spiritually instead of feeling sorry for yourself.

It prevents you from taking responsibility

Self-pity can lead to lack of self-awareness and an inability to learn from your mistakes. In this state of mind, people blame others for their issues. It must be realised that this is not a constructive behaviour. Instead, you should learn how to take responsibility for your own actions.

It prevents you from moving on

Self-pity is a sign that you are holding on to a past loss or trauma which does not let you move forward in life. If you are finding it difficult to move on, consider seeking help from mental health professionals who can help you work through these feelings and prosper in life.

It prevents you from finding happiness

When you are having excessive feelings of self-pity, you are not taking any productive or constructive action.

Hence, you will be stagnating in your life. Happiness only comes in those moments when you take decisive action in your life.

It makes it harder to take action

Self-pity can lead to feelings of helplessness and an inability to take meaningful action. You may feel as if you are stuck and not progressing. In this scenario, try taking small steps towards a goal which you would like to achieve.

It makes you bitter

Self-pity can lead to bitterness, which is a form of anger that is directed at yourself or others. Here, it is important to focus on what you can do in the present moment instead of dwelling on the past.

It makes it harder to stay motivated

Self-pity can lead to apathy which in turn results in lack of motivation. Instead, try focussing on something that excites you and drives you towards achieving your goals.

It prevents you from growing

Self-pity when unchecked can keep you stuck in the same patterns, which prevent you from learning and growing as an individual. It leads to your stagnation. Instead, focus on challenging yourself and finding new ways to learn and grow.

Tips to control self-pity

So, now that we know about self-pity and how it is not a helpful emotion, let us look at ways on how to stop the spiral of self-pity before it gets out of control.

Learn when a downward spiral is starting

You may find yourself thinking "I am not good enough", or you may be avoiding activities you usually liked participating in. Once you have noticed this trend in your thoughts and actions, begin to take remedial action. Sometimes recognising the start of a downward spiral is enough to stop it. Learn to identify your normal state of mind and how you think and react when you are happy and content. When you identify thoughts that are out of the ordinary, you will know that you need to take action to limit the damage.

Face your feelings

There is a reason you are feeling self-pity. Take time to realise and accept that grief, disappointment and loneliness are all normal feelings. Try writing about your feelings in a journal and analyse what they are trying to tell you. The only way to get through negative emotions is to feel them, work through them and let them pass.

Forgive yourself for your mistakes

When you are feeling self-pity, it is easy and normal to focus on the bad. Acknowledge and accept that you are not perfect. Cut yourself some slack for your imperfections. When you do so, you will realise that your mistakes and imperfections are not as bad as you think they are.

Write yourself a reminder

Write something you need to remind yourself of and put it somewhere you will see it often. For example, write "you are good enough" and stick it on the front of your study table. This positive reaffirmation will do wonders to your sense of confidence and self-worth.

Think about the situation as an opportunity to grow

Find meaning in the situation that caused your downward spiral. Analyse what went wrong and what caused it. While it is difficult to think about your situation optimistically when you are in a downward spiral, try to look at the moment as an opportunity to challenge yourself and grow.

Avoid situations that make you feel bad about yourself

Once you identify and recognise situations and/or people that can start a downward spiral for you, avoid them altogether. Do not be afraid of setting boundaries. Doing so will only help your sense of self-confidence and stop your self-pity.

List your strengths and achievements

List out the wins that you have had. It does not matter if they are big or small. Write down things that you like about yourself and things that you do well. Remind yourself of your positive qualities. Keep a designated journal for listing your positive moments, features and events.

Focus on your hygiene and physical activity

When you are feeling down or low, it is easy to neglect taking care of yourself. But remember that these simple actions can build your self-confidence. Brush your teeth, take a shower and do a workout.

Eat a healthy diet

A healthy diet is vital for your mental and physical well-being. Nourish your body with adequate nutritious foods, and as far as possible, avoid fast food, sugary drinks and processed foods.

Get enough sleep

You are at your best when you are relaxed. And to be relaxed you need to be well rested, which involves getting at least seven to eight hours of uninterrupted sleep every night. Set a bedtime and wake-up time for yourself so that it becomes part of your routine.

Practise gratitude

Start a gratitude journal and list down things that you are thankful for. Big or small, write down one thing every day that makes you grateful. This will help you start looking for positive things every day.

Do something helpful for others

If you have the time and energy, you can try volunteering opportunities. Doing something good for others need not take much time and at the end of the activity you will definitely feel happier about yourself.

Start your day with some positivity

Begin your day with repeating positive affirmations to yourself. You may find it strange at the beginning, but over a period of time, such affirmations will fill you with feelings of confidence and positive self-worth.

Keep complaining to a minimum

When you are feeling low, you may have the urge to complain about the situation which is causing your internal turmoil. However, this can actually make you feel worse. Complaining about it means that you are spending time thinking about the negative aspects of your situation instead of taking constructive action to make your way out of it. Also, distance yourself from negative people who constantly complain, as you may feel the urge to complain yourself.

Praise yourself for your success

When you feel self-pity, it is natural to minimise your accomplishments. So, learn to recognise and acknowledge the fact that you got out of bed and engaged in productive activities despite how you felt. Learn to give credit to yourself for all your wins, irrespective of whether they are big or small.

Developing mental strength requires time and consistent effort, just like when you want to build your physical strength. Everyone is capable of building their mental strength. By developing an increased ability to regulate your thoughts, manage your emotions and behave productively despite your circumstances, you will grow stronger and become more resilient.

10
You Got This!

Self-confidence can be defined as "confidence in yourself and your abilities". Your degree of self-confidence varies according to situation and also the area you are working on. For example, you may be confident in one subject of your studies while in other subjects you may need to do some work to get proficient. Research has shown that self-confidence is important for health and psychological well-being. Having a healthy level of self-confidence can help you become more successful in your personal and professional life. Research has also revealed that more confident people tend to achieve more academically and professionally.

Benefits of having self-confidence

There are several benefits of having a healthy degree of self-confidence. Let us look into each one of them in detail.

Better performance

You perform better at your tasks when you have confidence in yourself. Instead of wasting time and energy worrying whether you are good enough, you devote that energy towards your productive efforts.

Having healthier relationships

Having self-confidence not only impacts your own performance and how you feel about yourself, but also helps understand others better. It also gives you the strength and confidence to walk away from a relationship if you are not getting what you want or deserve.

Openness to try new things

When you believe in yourself, you find the confidence to try new things. Whether it be signing up for a cooking class or applying for that promotion you think you deserve, putting yourself out there is a lot easier when you have self-confidence and faith in your own abilities.

Being your best under stress

When you are confident, you will perform to the best of your abilities and fulfil your potential when it counts most, especially when under pressure.

Influencing others

Self-confident people often find it easier to influence others more readily. This helps especially when selling an idea or product or negotiating at work or home.

Having leadership and executive presence

Self-confidence plays a huge part in having leadership and executive presence. You create such presence by how you think, act, carry yourself and use your voice.

Exuding a more positive attitude

When you feel confident about yourself, you believe that you are important and have a vital and meaningful place in the world.

Reducing the impact of negative thoughts

While negative thoughts will always be there in your mind, having a high degree of self-confidence will ensure that you are not negatively impacted by such thoughts. Someone with a low level of self-confidence can at times crumble under the weight of negative thoughts and feelings. When your self-confidence is at a healthy level, you will know how to deal with such thoughts and feelings in a mature way so that it does not negatively affect your work or mindset.

Experiencing more fearlessness and less anxiety

When you have confidence in your abilities, you know what you can do. Hence, it is easier for you to explore new horizons and surmount new challenges with reduced fear and anxiety. Your faith in your own abilities will ensure that you know how to deal with the issues that you may face along the way.

Having greater freedom from social anxiety

When you are confident, you are more comfortable with yourself and do not seek external validation. Thereby, you are not as concerned about what others think about you. How liberating!

Gaining motivation and energy to take action

Self-confidence gives you the impetus to take action towards achieving your personal and professional goals and dreams. The more energised and motivated you are, the more you are likely to take immediate actions towards your objectives.

Being happier

Confident people usually tend to be happier and more satisfied with their lives than people who lack self-confidence. This is because over a period of time, such people have taken positive and constructive action towards achieving their goals, which builds a sense of self-assurance and satisfaction, thereby leading to greater happiness.

Traits of a self-confident person

When learning how to be more confident, it is helpful to understand how someone with self-confidence is different from someone who is insecure. Here are some of the differences between the two.

Celebrates others' success

Confident people do not get envious of anyone else's success.

Open-minded

Such people are open-minded and always open to new views that broaden their horizons and knowledge.

Optimistic

Optimism is one of the hallmarks of confident people. They believe in having a positive attitude.

Willingness to take risks

As confident people are assured about their own abilities, they can regularly step out of their comfort zones and expand their horizons. They are always hungry for growth and challenge themselves to explore and conquer new frontiers.

Laugh at themselves

Confident people have the wonderful quality of being able to laugh at themselves. They are loved and cherished by their peer group because of their ability to laugh even when they are the butt of a joke. At times, they will also crack jokes at their own expense. Such a quality comes only when the person is self-assured. People with confidence issues may easily get offended when someone makes fun of them.

Decisive

Confident people have their future path planned and laid out in their minds. They know exactly what they want, what is important to them and what is of no value. Hence, they are inherently decisive people.

Always learning and growing

Confident people look at chances to learn as opportunities for self-growth. They look forward to such moments eagerly. They realise that learning and growth never truly stops and life involves constant exchange of valuable knowledge.

Admits mistakes

Confident people are extremely self-aware. They know when they have erred and admit to their mistakes. When they make mistakes, confident people make a note of what went wrong and why they made the mistake they did. By doing so, they ensure that they do not make the same mistake once again.

Accepts responsibility

With a high degree of self-assurance and confidence comes the ability to accept responsibility. Confident people are usually at the forefront when it comes to taking action and making new innovations. They accept the responsibility for the task and plan and execute their plans to ensure that they emerge successful at completing the job.

Tips for being more self-confident

So, how is it possible to build your level of confidence and become more self-assured? Let's dive in and find out.

Stop comparing yourself to others

Ask yourself if you have the habit of comparing yourself to others. It can be comparing the number of Instagram followers you have, the salary you earn or even the marks you got in the latest examination. While comparing yourself to others is a natural part of human behaviour, remember that doing so will hurt your self-confidence. Research has shown that when people compare themselves to others, they experience envy. And the more envy they have, the worse they feel about themselves. Here, it must be noted that if you look at yourself in a negative way, it affects the level of faith you have in your own abilities. This in turn will hamper your performance when you undertake tasks. So, as far as possible avoid comparing yourself to others.

Surround yourself with positive people

Take a moment to take stock of how your friends make you feel. Do they lift you up or do they bring you down? Are they supportive of you or do they constantly judge you? Do they accept you for who you are? The people you spend time with can have a big influence on your thoughts and attitudes about yourself. So, pay attention to how they make you feel. If you believe that their presence is negative and that they do not add value to your life, it may be time to say goodbye to them. Instead, surround yourself with people who genuinely and truly love you and want you to do well in life. Connect and interact with people with qualities which you wish to have and learn to incorporate these habits and qualities into your life and mindset.

Take care of your body

Research has shown that if you feel good physically, you will usually feel great in your mind. To maintain good physical health, you must have a balanced and healthy diet, exercise regularly, meditate and have good quality sleep on a regular basis. Caring for your body is an integral part of self-confidence. It makes sure that your body gets what it needs so that you feel good about yourself and your abilities.

Be kind to yourself

Self-compassion involves treating yourself with kindness when you make a mistake, fail or experience a setback. It helps you connect with yourself on a deeper level so that you can navigate through challenging emotions. Research has shown a deep connection between self-compassion and self-confidence. So the next time you are faced with a challenging situation, give it your best shot, while at the same time recognising that being imperfect or falling short is part and parcel of being a human being. Do your best to navigate through the challenging situations with compassion towards yourself.

Practise positive self-talk

Self-talk that is positive and optimistic can foster self-compassion and help you overcome self-doubt and take on new challenges with confidence and gusto. Negative self-talk can limit your abilities and lessen your confidence. Self-talk is a very vital part of your mental well-being. Learn to identify when your self-talk becomes negative and take corrective action as soon as you realise it. When you do so, you will stop it from progressing into something more serious. When you start practising positive self-talk, barriers and obstacles which earlier seemed insurmountable will start looking manageable. You will get the boost in confidence to give it a shot.

Face your fears

Stop putting things off till you feel more confident. One of the best ways to build confidence is by facing your fears head-on. Practise facing your fears that stem from a lack of self-confidence. Try anyway and do not let feelings of inadequacy stop you in your quest. Tell yourself that it is an experiment and see what happens. You will learn that being a little anxious or making a few mistakes is not as bad as you thought initally. Each time you move forward and challenge yourself, you will gain more confidence in yourself and your abilities.

Know when to say no

Setting social and emotional boundaries enables you to feel safer psychologically. It can help you feel more in control of yourself. Boundaries help establish this feeling of control.

Set realistic goals

Pursuing goals often involves failing several times until you figure out what works. At times, this can make you wonder if you have what it takes to succeed. It can also lead you to question how you can be more self-confident while still achieving your dreams. Setting high and lofty goals and failing to achieve them is a sure-shot way of damaging your confidence levels. Conversely, realistic goals are achievable. And the more you achieve your goals, the greater will be your confidence in yourself and your abilities. To set realistic goals, write down what you want to achieve. Next, honestly ask yourself what chance you have of attaining it. If the answer is slim to none, the goal may be too lofty. In this situation, dial it back a bit to make the goal more realistic and achievable. This may require you to do some amount of research. When you know how to achieve what you want to, you can get to work, and once you accomplish your goal, it will boost your self-confidence.

Everyone struggles with issues of confidence now and then. This is completely normal. However, what must be noted is that the dip in confidence should be temporary and not prolonged. If it continues over a substantial period of time, it may lead to issues like anxiety or even depression. So, learn to identify when your lack of confidence interferes with your studies, work or social life, and if required, take the help of a mental health professional. You have come a long way to achieve whatever you have so far. Be happy about that and pat yourself on the back. Remember those moments when you put in effort and emerged successful. Reliving those times will reinvigorate you and give you the impetus to take on new challenges. And finally, never forget to engage in positive self-talk. Anytime you are doubting yourself, remember the past instances when you overcame seemingly insurmountable challenges and tell yourself, "You got this!"

Your Thoughts